T0144972

Good Bless You

GOOD

Written & Illustrated by:
Barbara Ann Mack

Balboa Press books may be ordered through booksellers or by contacting:

Balboa Press
A Division of Hay House
1663 Liberty Drive
Bloomington, IN 47403
www.balboapress.com
1 (877) 407-4847

Because of the dynamic nature of the Internet, any web addresses or links contained in this book may have changed since publication and may no longer be valid. The views expressed in this work are solely those of the author and do not necessarily reflect the views of the publisher, and the publisher hereby disclaims any responsibility for them.

Any people depicted in stock imagery provided by Getty Images are models, and such images are being used for illustrative purposes only. Certain stock imagery © Getty Images.

ISBN: 978-1-9822-2241-3 (sc)
ISBN: 978-1-9822-2242-0 (e)

Library of Congress Control Number: 2019902126

Print information available on the last page.

Balboa Press rev. date: 03/20/2019

BALBOA PRESS
A DIVISION OF HAY HOUSE

"Welcome to a life provoking read!

There are pages at the conclusion of this book that you may fined
to be helpful to jot down or illustrate your
thoughts, feelings and question that may come up.

I suggest you embrace them all. Let them guide you! Don't try to
implement them, or run from them! "

Hello! Most High Being breathing Now with me.

I'm so glad we're expressing all the good that's meant to be.

Together we're releasing worn out figuring and fear.

And embracing from the spaces the whimsical and surreal.

Thoughts and feelings, words and colors, gladly dance onto the page.

So the party! Good Bless You can find its home on the world's stage.

Things are bursting, popping, and unfolding for me.
Right now, while I'm sitting here contemplating.
In the air, on the waves, beyond 20/20 sight.
Good news, great breaks, miracles in flight.

Yes, yes, and amen; its most certainly true.
You can bank on the good coming directly to you.
The universe produces from its bag of tricks.
So your thoughts become things through this happening matrix.

What a trip! What a party! What a blast this can be.
Watching for the blessings I'm surely bound to receive.
What kind? Which color? How many suit me best?
Well, I'm sorting through choices til my clarity rests.

Oh it's fun, such a pleasure to choose and define
All the health, wealth, and circumstances soon to be mine.
And what's best about this, is we do it together.
My family is the world; we all help each other.

Well, _____, I love you all the while you are today.
Right now, every hour, I'm realizing all I may.
Expanding, enlarging, allowing mOrE to be.
I am giving. I'm expressing the flow of Life! through me.

It feels so good. It feels so great!
To know my future's a happy fate. ☺

Goodness tweaks my thoughts til my heart forms a song.
My delights and desires build the beat loud and strong.
The "how" of the universe digs the rhythm that it feels.
And the Now jazzed with power offers up the surreal.

That's me and the universe seeing it through.
I choose my thoughts; It manages the crew.
And they bring it, I tell you, happily with ease.
Aiming to fashion exactly what I please.

Fifty's, hundred's, thousand's and such.
Drawn to my fingers — easy to touch.
Charming, helpful, and pleasant are they.
Here at my service now and always.

Filling my account today and each week.
What is normal to me, to others is Greek.
It's building and boosting and blessing my sphere.
Money's good and there's plenty for all of us here.

I'm filled with the feeling abundance now brings —
Gratefulness, thankfulness and appreciating.
I remember the origin, the beginning, the start —
My twinkling thoughts from a happy heart.

FEAR → ? ! ? ! ?

WAIT A MINUTE "rational" thinking demands a say.
Isn't it ridiculous to carry on this way.
You can see with your eyes and hear with your ears
Breaking news of the day escalating "The Fear."

"The Fear" it is happening throughout human kind
As it magnifies the horizontal cares of the mind.
The thought of this world is worshiped with glee
Through our minds, on our lips and in our actions finally.

It crosses all cultures, all regions, all time.
Soon after the Beginning we fostered its climb
By forgetting the Life and its flow, its worth
And myopically calculating our way on this earth.

Here we are, the Creation, standing in this age
With the choice to continue or to Otherwise engage.
A fresh take, on the false start, which dominated our dust
Threatening the mother lode of a civilization bust.

Re-wick your lamps so good light shines its rays
Transmuting what is, to the answer for these days.
Trust your internal, eternal, fully conscious view.
It will powerfully, peacefully re-write the world news.

But it starts with your "treasure," your "log," your "take."
Focus on the good and give the world a break.
Practice finding good in your home, at your work.
And let the yeast multiply til goodness just bursts.

Into loving and healing in heart, hands, and home,
Massaging caustic attitudes in to welcoming ones.
Your finances, your body, your life purpose will ignite
With the trickle down power of goodness minus fight.

GOOD

So "The Fear" rightly orphaned can no longer abide.
See "The Light" it's now beaming from my inside.
Pass it on — the Good News — from part to part,
Til it fills all my soul, restoring my heart.

Flowing in, around, over and through
Warming, and feeding, and cleansing is the Truth.
Good: sprouting, spreading, and rooting new thoughts
Which are building good things in my body, on my block.

It's catchy, the good stuff, if I let it grow.
Catch the end of each good thought and smile, "Let's go."
Then follow it happily as it makes its OWN path.
And don't bother to question or to figure the math.

Goodness is expanding all throughout
As my members are cheering and shifting about.
Oh, I feel it, and sense it, before I see.
How thinking on goodness rearranges me.

My cells are quite happily chatting together.
Inspiring my organs to chant, "we're recovered!"
My blood, as it circulates making the rounds
Is spreading the JOY in leaps and bounds.

Fluid, flexible, bending at will.
Swallowing, running and cycling up hill,
Digesting and functioning just the right way.
My body is a pleasure to live in today.

I'm filled with the feeling well-being now brings;
Gratitude, thankfulness, and appreciating.
And I feel so good that I just want to shout
"Hey, everybody. Let your good come out!"

This mysterious Good which is housed in each frame
Also travels at large making more of the same.
It is nestled in the matter of our activity each day
Waiting to be acknowledged and wooed out into play.

The Good has its own methods and you must give it free reign.
To bring into your experience things and people you may disdain.
Initially, I don't like it; it disturbs my way of being.
It messes with my mind and rocks my view of e-v-e-r-y-t-h-i-n-g!

What's normal gets all weird and the usual doesn't fly.
Cause anOther way is birthing and it's one I've never tried.
The Voice is like none other that I've ever let rule me.
It's rich, and light, and freeing and it feels so fresh and clean.

Despite my "ah ha" moments and the aliveness that I feel
I question and I wonder if this Other way is the real deal.
It seems too plain and simple to be the answer for which I've sought.
For anyone with eyes to see and ears to hear it can be caught.

For anyone who's hungry for a rest and a reprieve,
The Good is all over, everywhere, just waiting to be perceived.
I am an "anyone" enjoying this Other life that I now know.
It feels so right and inviting that I'm sure I'm finally Home.

So I'm filled with the feeling belonging now brings;
Gratitude, thankfulness, and appreciating.
And I wish for fellow travelers who bear a heavy load
To see the Good inside themselves and more out upon the road.

For my yoke is easy; my burden is light.
Acknowledging Good makes my steps go right.
I K(now) the way to the place that I go —
By looking inside and by feeling my soul.

And it feels so good from every angle.
Goodness beams warmth releasing all tangles.
My past is all finished; my future's all clear.
So my thoughts become things in this rich atmosphere.

Nothing restricting, controlling, holding back,
Delicious, refreshing, all new and no lack.
Goodness through me, a new world it will build.
As I freely choose from the creative field.

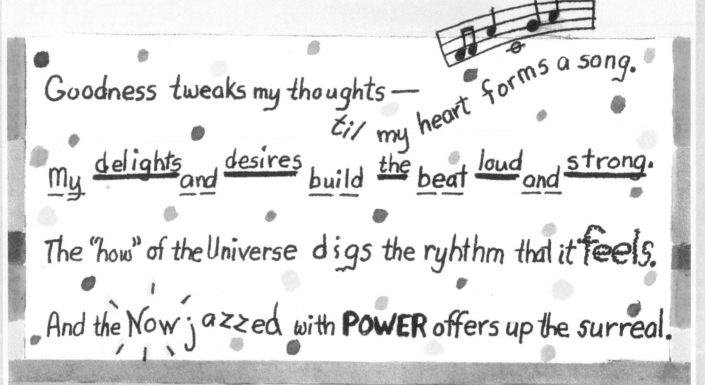

Goodness tweaks my thoughts —
                    til my heart forms a song.
My delights and desires build the beat loud and strong.

The "how" of the Universe digs the ryhthm that it feels.

And the Now jazzed with **POWER** offers up the surreal.

BAM

2010 Storm Lake, Iowa

NOTES

NOTES

NOTES AND ILLUSTRATIONS

_____

_____

_____

_____

_____

_____

_____

_____

NOTES AND ILLUSTRATIONS

_____

_____

_____

_____

_____

_____

_____

_____

NOTES AND ILLUSTRATIONS

_____

_____

_____

_____

_____

_____

_____

_____

About the Author

Barbara (Fountain) Mack was born in rural Iowa. She received an Interdisciplinary Degree in the Humanities from the University of Northern Iowa. In her junior year she submitted a term paper entitled "Pleasing the Self," in which she synthesized a semester's class information into an inter related, multi-level view point. Her professors were amazed, and her curiosity was piqued at the possibility and benefit of this interdisciplinary view of common life experiences.

In the next years, working for a nonprofit, career education organization in metropolitan New Jersey, she garnered experience from interfacing with politics and fund raising, corporate power structures, school systems: rural to inner city and image building at a personal and professional level. Later, as a dorm supervisor for seven years at a religious institution, she added multi-national relationships as well as employee and student mediation. For more than a year Barbara engaged in life studies for inmates at a maximum security women's prison.

Barbara has always journaled, categorized, philosophized and re-adjusted her world view, reaching for a positive yet realistic outlook. Good Bless You percolated out of her life experiences. Her second book, I AM, follows as a practical companion.

She and her husband, Ted, and their teenage daughters, Martha Anne and Susan, live in sunny, southern California with their dog, Jack, and their cat, Mr. Daisy.

Printed in the United States
By Bookmasters